UNSEEN

akin olunloyo

SYNCTERFACE
Syncterface Media
London
www.syncterfacemedia.com

UNSEEN
A Book of Inspired Lyrics and Rhymes

ISBN: 978-1-912896-27-1

Copyright © December 2021

akin olunloyo

Published in the United Kingdom by

SYNCTERFACE™

Syncterface Media, London
www.syncterfacemedia.com
info@syncterfacemedia.com

Cover Design
Syncterface Media, London

This book is printed on acid-free paper

To
Beautiful Betty
&
Handsome Bruce

I still miss you like crazy

Contents

Intro

*I*t all started while I was in uni. I had been through an unplanned life-changing experience, but nothing seemed to have changed. A few friends of mine had been through something similar, and they had miraculously started doing things they claimed they couldn't do before. So, was I the problem?

Anyway, one lovely evening I decided to do something I hardly ever did; pop into one of the lecture rooms to actually do some studying. It was a strange feeling because everyone, including myself, knew that any reading I was going to get done usually happened in my room, on my bed.

I should have known it would be one of those evenings when I walked into an empty room that normally should have been packed with students. "Where was everybody?" I thought. Was something going down that I didn't know about? I spent a few moments contemplating if I should stay or not and finally decided on the former. As I took a seat in the classroom, all alone, I found myself pondering: As a Christian, was I really all alone?

After my recent spiritual experience, I was told that even though I might not notice anything different on the outside, a change had definitely happened on my inside. Also, though I hadn't totally grasped it yet, I knew that the One I had given my life to happened to be in all places at all times. So, though I was alone, I actually wasn't. The thought brought a smile to my face.

At about the same time, I felt the sudden urge to pick up my pen and start writing. Now, this was crazy simply because writing was one thing I kinda hated doing. If not for the fact that I had to get an education, I could have done without it. But there I was in a room all alone, yet not alone, putting my pen to paper and writing, and about 15 minutes later, I had written my very first poem called "A Job To Do". The scary part was that I didn't have to think about it; it just seemed to flow naturally. Now, don't get me wrong, it didn't exactly include any fancy words or anything like that, but it actually made sense. It also made me realise that it didn't have that much to do with me.

Well, ever since that day, I've never stopped writing, and after what God dropped in my heart in the winter of 1991, which was confirmed on the 19th of February 1994 when my team and I met up with Graham Kendrick, I guess I never will.

So, here are a few unseen words I have written over the last 30 plus years. Sit back, relax and enjoy the simplicity of poetry that has little to do with me.

~ akin olunloyo

Foreword

When I first met Akin about 30 years ago, one of the first things that struck me was his gift for writing. He would write songs, poems and rhymes at the drop of a hat. So, when he asked me to write the foreword to this book, I was very honoured.

This book of rhymes and poems is a book ANYONE and EVERYONE would love. It's an easy read filled with words of encouragement for us and words of praise and love to our Father. It serves as a reminder of God's faithfulness, power and grace. It also reminds us of His awesome love when He gave His life for us on Calvary. Some of these words have been put to music and are songs we sing today.

This is a labour of love of words written over more than 30 years. It's just the sort of book you want to pick up on a rainy day when you're curled up under your duvet. It's also the book you want to read on a busy, hectic day when you just need a little encouragement.

I have thoroughly enjoyed going through these poems and rhymes, and I am sure you will too. It will brighten up your darkest day and make a joyous one even better.

This book is definitely one to read again and again, and I am certain it will bless you just as much as it has blessed me.

Thank you, Akin, for letting us have a peep into this awesome gift that God has given you.

~ *Debisi Olunloyo*

Have Your Way

Lord, have Your way in my life today
May I do the things that You say,
As I lean upon Your Spirit
May I glorify Your name
This is my prayer:
Have Your Way

Lord, I want to walk in Your ways
Shine as Your light every day
All I want to do
Is what You ask me to
Lord, I surrender all to You;
Have Your Way

I Come

I come before Your throne
And Lord I bow,
I honour, I adore,
I praise You now;
True worship from my heart
O Lord, I bring
I give my heart to You
As an offering

Give You Praise

O loving God
You broke the chains of sin,
I give You praise;
You gave me life
So I might live again,
I give You praise

Your mercy
I just cannot comprehend,
I give You praise;
Your love for me
I know it has no end,
I give You praise

Lord, I give You praise
I adore Your name
Forever the same
I give You praise

Wonderful, Marvellous
Beautiful, Glorious
Merciful in all Your ways
Your great name I praise

Lord, I give You praise
I adore Your name
Forever the same
I give You praise

For Who You Are

When Your praises go up
I know Your blessings come down,
But today, Lord, I praise You
For who You are

You're Alpha, Omega
My loving life-giver
So faithful,
No one can compare;
Awesome, so wonderful,
Mighty, so powerful,
Maker of all things
You are the King of kings

So, I praise You for who You are
Jehovah, the mighty God;
Worthy of honour
Worthy of glory
Worthy of praise forever

Lift Your Name

Holy one of Israel
There is none like You
You're the King and Lord of all
None can do what You do

Father, You are my hiding place
My shelter from the storm
I find rest in Your saving grace
You're my everything, my all

So, I lift Your name on high
With a heart of adoration
I lift Your name on high
With a voice of declaration
I lift Your name on high
O Lord, You're my salvation
Forever and always
I lift Your name on high

How Excellent

When I wake up in the morning
To the fulness of the day
I get this soothing feeling
Like a shining sunlight ray;
It sinks right through my ceiling
To the depths of my soul
And somewhere deep inside
This one thing I know

A touch of Your hand is all I need
To know that I'll make it through the day
As long as I hear Your voice to lead
I'm guaranteed to go all the way

When the sun has gone to sleep
In the middle of the night,
In the midst of all the darkness
The moon keeps shining bright;
It reminds me of Your presence
In a world that is so bleak
How, when I'm feeling lonely
I know You're there with me

Times when I'm down and low, I know
You're going to lift me up again
And fill my heart with joy and hope
And strength for yet another day

How excellent is Your name in all the earth
You're amazing;
You shine so bright;
How excellent is Your name in all the earth
There could never be another
That could ever love me like You do;
No one else can love me like You!

Glory and Honour

Glory and honour
Dominion and strength
Belong to the King of kings
Who created the heavens,
Created the earth,
And every living thing

So, we lift up our voices
And sing hallelujah,
Lord, there is none like You
You're so wonderful, powerful
Faithful and true,
There's nothing You can't do;
Lord, we worship You
From our hearts today

Worship we bring
As our offering
O Lord,
We adore You;
Worship we bring
Your praises we sing
O Lord,
There's no one like You

My Heavenly Father

My Heavenly Father,
Awesome is Your name
You're wonderful, so powerful
The Ancient of all days;
Who can do the things You do?
I could search, but none I'll find;
My Heavenly Father
You're truly one of a kind

Ogo Ye O

Oba aye ra ye
Oruko re lo tobi ju
Ni gbogbo agbaye
Ta lo le se inkan ti Wo se
You healed the sick, You raised the dead
Made the blind to see
You bruised the devil's head;
Oba aye ra ye
Iwo logo ye

Ogo ye O o
Iyin ye O o
Ope ye O o
Eledumare

Jesus, You're the mighty One
King of kings and Lord of lords
Nothing is too hard for You to do
You hold the key to every breakthrough;
Awa gbe oruko re ga
Iwo ni Olorun ara
Oba aye ra ye
Iwo logo ye

Ogo ye O o
Iyin ye O o
Ope ye O o
Eledumare

Worthy

Worthy, worthy, worthy
Are You, Lord
Worthy, are You, Lord

You're worthy of glory
You're worthy of the praise
So mighty, full of mercy
The Ancient of all days;
I could search through all eternity
But none like You I'll find
Forever You're the same
Lord, I bless Your holy name

Worthy, worthy, worthy
Are You, Lord
Worthy, are You, Lord

You Reign

Almighty God,
You are the Holy One
And Your faithfulness extends to the clouds
So far above
The highest peaks
Cannot be compared
With the greatness of Your love;
Almighty God,
You reign forevermore

None Like You

Who is there Like You O Lord
In the heavens and the earth
Faithful and true, merciful too;
Who is there Like You O Lord
In the heavens and the earth
Father,
There is none like You

We join the elders and the angels
And bow before Your throne,
All the universe declare Your praise;
You're high and lifted O God
Your glory floods this place,
Lord, there is none,
No one like You

Who is there Like You O Lord
In the heavens and the earth
Faithful and true, merciful too;
Who is there Like You O Lord
In the heavens and the earth
Father,
There is none like You

Forever the Same

You may be facing
A mountain of great height
You've knelt down in prayer,
And God's told you it will be alright;
But the days keep ticking by;
The future looks so bleak,
The answer seems so far away
And your faith begins to leak

But remember what God told you,
He's always by your side,
If He says that He will do something
He's God; He never lies;
So, put your trust in Him alone;
He'll come through once again
Yesterday, today, forever
Our God is forever the same

It doesn't matter the situation
Or how scary it may seem
God is always listening
You mean so much to Him;
So, when the devil tells you,
Your wait is in vain,
Never doubt the Almighty;
He is never late

He is just, and He is faithful,
So caring, and so kind;
His love is never-ending;
He's forgiving all the time;
Put your trust in Him alone
And He will heal your pain;
Yesterday, today, forever
Our God is forever the same

He is the Almighty
And He will never change
As He was with the saints of old
He is with you today;
He will never forsake you
In His word, He makes it plain
He's a God of loving-kindness
And He's forever the same

My.. Everything

How can I begin to say
The way I feel about Your love;
The way You saved me
When You took me
From the miry clay

You gave Your life for me on the tree,
Shed Your blood to set me free
There could never be another like You;
No one else can love me like You do

The first, the last, the everything in between
That is what You mean to me;
You are everything to me

You looked beyond my every sin
You sent Your love to rescue me,
I could never repay
But I thank You

I was so blind couldn't see the day
But you took my hand
And showed me the way;
Where would I be
If Your love hadn't found me?

The first, the last, the everything in between
That is what You mean to me;
You are everything to me

My beginning, my end,
My everything
My Father, my Friend,
My everything
My Alpha, my Omega,
My everything
My Saviour, Creator,
My everything
Protector, Provider,
My everything
My Healer, Deliverer,
My everything
My Selfless, life-giver,
My everything
Never changing God,
My everything
Ever-loving God,
My everything
Never failing God,
My everything
Ever faithful God,
My everything

Everything to Me

Lord, You gave Your precious life for me
Lord, You shed Your precious blood for me
Lord, You rose that I may live
My every sin Your love forgives

Exchanged my weakness with Your strength
Replaced my sickness , took away my pain;
Though You were rich, You became poor
You changed my life forevermore

You are the rock of my salvation
My Chief Cornerstone
You are my sure foundation
With You, I'm never alone
My loving Redeemer
In You, I find true peace
My beginning and my end
You're everything to me

All My Days

JESUS,
You came and died for me
JESUS,
You came and set me free
From the hold of the evil one
From the grasp of the enemy
And now I am complete
Thanks to shed blood at Calvary

A temple of God's Spirit
That's what I am today
More than a conqueror
I grow stronger in You each day;
I meditate upon Your word
It sets my path aright,
And I conform to Your image
More and more, day and night

My Saviour, my Redeemer
I'll praise You all my days
With all that is within me
I'll follow in Your ways;
I honour and adore You
To You, I'm truly grateful
I'll worship You always
I'll praise You all my days

A Brand New Day!

The cock crows
The morning breaks
Another sunrise
A brand new day!

Rays of wisdom flood your heart
The scent of favour fills the air
As a new day of opportunities
Once again takes a stare

It says,
"I'm not the same as yesterday
I've got so much more in store.
What are you going to do with me?
I don't have to be like the day before."

What are you going to make of today?
Its destiny lies in your hands
You can use it to make the world better
Or simply stare and stand

You can surge ahead or stay in bed
It's a choice that's yours to make
But remember, old things are history
Today's a brand new day!

Yet Another Day!

The cock crows
The morning breaks
Another sunrise
Yet another day!

Rays of light hit your eyes
Your lashes begin to flutter
Thoughts scroll across your screen
Like words on a computer:

Same as yesterday! The message reads
Your tired yawn tells the story;
But does it have to be the same old cycle?
You could try something new, surely

There's more to life than waking up
And living out a routine
Why not step out of that comfort zone
And try something amazing

Life could be much more fulfilling,
Fulfilling in so many ways
If you only woke up not thinking
Agh, yet another day!

He Cares

With Father, there's always a way
It doesn't matter what you face;
Forsake you or leave you,
He'll never do
Through thick and thin,
He'll always stand by you

With you, He is always present
He knows your needs before you present
So, put your trust in Him each day
And He'll lead you in His loving ways

Our Father is just and He is faithful
Caring, loving and merciful;
So, the troubles, the worries, the pain you bear
Cast it on Him because, for you,
He cares!

You Alone

There is none like my God
There is none like my King
You alone are worthy of my praise;
I come, and I adore You
I bow and glorify You
You alone are worthy of my praise

You are my Saviour
You're my Deliverer
You alone are worthy of my praise;
You're my Shelter
My Strong Tower
You alone are worthy of my praise

Without You

I'd be lost and forlorn
Without You
No wiser than a fool
Without You
I would have lost the fight
Without You in my life

I wouldn't have a smiling face
Without You
No sun, lots of rain
Without You
Hope, a distant cry
Without You in my life

Life wouldn't be the same
Without You
No love to make a change
Without You
Joy, out of sight
Without You in my life

But you turned my life around
The day I let You in
You filled my heart with love
You made life worth living;
Always by my side, through thick and through thin,
Where would I be if You weren't living within?
There's one thing I never want to do
And that's to live my life
Without You!

All in All

My strength and fortress
In You, I find rest
My help in time of need;
My shield, my buckler
My Lord, my Saviour
I humbly bow my knees

My strong tower
So full of power
In You, I place my trust;
You shine so brightly
In the midst of darkness
You give me hope when I'm lost

So, every day I'll fix my gaze on You
Living my life the way You want me to
Doing the things that You ask me to
Because You are my Lord, my everything

You are my all in all
My everything and so much more
No one else can do me like You do;
You are my all in all
The One I'm living for;
You mean more than this world to me
You're my all in all!

Hey, Child

Hey child,
How are you doing?
It's been a while
So I thought I'd come a-knocking;
We don't talk like we used to
But I know what you're going through;
About the hurt and the pain,
the heartaches;
About the stormy, rainy days,
The heartbreaks,
I'm right here if you need someone to talk to
It's Me; I'm always with you

Hey child,
I just want you to know
I'm never going to let you go
Because I really love you so;
Hey child,
I'm never going to wave goodbye
I'll always be by your side
So hold on,
Trust Me; you'll get by

I know you feel like no one understands
All alone, no one to hold your hand
But in Me, you have a friend
Who will love you to the end;
I know the number of hairs on your head,
I've got your name written on My palm,
And one thing I can't deny
Is that you're the apple of My eye

Hey child,
I just want you to know
I'm never going to let you go
Because I really love you so;
Hey child,
I'm never going to wave goodbye
I'll always be by your side
So hold on,
Trust Me; you'll get by

One, two
Hey child, I've missed you;
Three, four
That's why I'm knocking on your door;
Five to ten
I'm your forever friend
And I will love you to the end

Apple of His Eye

No matter what I face each day
My Father always makes a way
He lifts me when I'm feeling low
He comforts me when I'm all alone;
He calls me the head
When I feel like the tail
He says I'm a success
When it looks like I'll fail;
He picks me up whenever I fall
He hears my cry each time I call
He never leaves or forsakes me;
In me, He abides
He loves me unconditionally;
I am the apple of His eye

Healing Power

As I closed the dark squeaky gate
My heart beat at an alarming rate;
I thought I'd prayed that she'd be healed
That with Your power she'd be filled;
But after the call I made today
It was clear; she wasn't okay

But I'm not moved by the devil's lie
The prayer of faith is still alive,
And though inside I feel the pain
I know Father heard me when I prayed

So, by the stripes of Jesus
You are healed
From head to toe
Your healing is sealed;
I believe it; I've received it
And I know you have too;
So, devil, you lost again
Her healing just came through

Because He Came

"The future's so bleak"
That's what they say
And it's true,
Looking at the world today,
But though life's path may seem a little rough
Christ in me is more than enough

And when I think about Jesus' suffering
Everything He's done for me:
He came, He died, shed His blood on the tree
That I may live victoriously

So, in the midst of life's problems
The answer lies within;
With Christ in me
I am destined to win

Just because He came
I'm more than a conqueror
Because He came
Failure isn't mine anymore
Because He came
I'm one with the Father once again
And I will always overcome
Just because He came

God's Vessel

God may ask you to do something
And you may say, "That's impossible."
But, in your mind, don't limit His abilities
Just chill and let Him use you as
…His vessel

Many may criticise you,
But, they don't understand what God told you;
So, don't focus on the distraction
Just chill and let Him use you as
...His vessel

You are God's vessel
Made and fashioned by Him
To do the things He asks of you
To glorify His name;
You are God's vessel
Made to shine for Him
The road won't always be easy
But with Him,
You're destined to win

Child of the King

Like a hungry lion, the enemy roars
Looking for someone to devour
Tests and tribulations, trials of all sorts
he brings your way to make you fall

But, you've got all it takes to win
The Greater One lives within
So go ahead, lean on Him
Remember, you're a child of the King

When failure knocks on your door
And it seems you've lost the fight
Don't give up; hold on tight
In Him, your future is more than bright

You've got all it takes to win
The Greater One lives within
So go ahead, lean on Him
Remember, you're a child of the King

So, in times when the path looks so dark
And walking in faith seems so hard
He promises to carry your every care
So lean on Him; there's no need to fear

You've got all it takes to win
The Greater One lives within
So go ahead, lean on Him
Remember, you're a child of the King

I Met You

I was playing life away until I met You
Didn't know that I had strayed until I met You,
Then You opened up Your floodgates
Of mercy and compassion,
You took me in Your arms and told me
Your love for me is forever

Never knew about true peace until I met You
Didn't know what real love was until I met You,
But You came into my heart and showed me
All that I was missing,
You poured Your love inside of me
And filled me till I was dripping

Life is not the same now that I've met You
My talk, my walk has changed since I met You,
Now I'm strolling down a path so lovely
With the help of Your Holy Spirit
I never want to stray again
I'll gladly stay within Your limits

You turned my life around for good
You made me new
You gave me hope and joy afresh
Like no one else could do;
I'm surrounded by a love
So pure, so true,
And it's all because
I met You!

Alone No More

There are times along the way
When the going gets real tough;
Times when hope seems out of sight
And the path a little rough

Situations try to knock you down
Try to fill you up with fear;
Well, that's the devil doing his thing
But remember, God is near

You've got all it takes to win
The Holy Spirit within
So though the devil may roar
Never forget,
You're alone no more

Yep, you're alone no more
But there's still something you can't ignore;
The devil's around seeking someone to devour
Tempting with temptations to try and make you fall

he'll knock on your door with evil plans
But don't worry, the power's in your hands
Will you let him in or leave him outside?
It's about time you made up your mind

Remember, it's a spiritual war
Your power and might won't work anymore,
But lean on the One who lives in you
With Him, there's nothing you can't do

You're an overcomer
And so much more
Simply because
You're alone no more

Thank You

I was lost; I was down real low
Kept walking, didn't know where to go;
Thought I had a plan for the life I was living
Thought I could make it without believing

But I was wrong,
Each day grew darker;
I needed a little light
To turn my sadness into laughter;
I needed Somebody to show me the way,
I needed Someone who wouldn't hesitate

And like a shining star
You shone through my heart
And promised to love me eternally;
I can live with no clothes
Or no food to eat
But I can't live without You beside me!

I was blind, but now I see
Since that day, You rescued me
Lifted me when I was sinking
Shone Your light, and now I'm smiling

Every day and every night
Sweet memories of You flood my mind;
Ways You touch my heart,
So hard to comprehend
I just want to say, "Thank You."
For being my True Friend

Thank You
For giving me a brand new start
Thank You
For living inside my heart
Thank You
For giving me a life to live
Thank You
For the unconditional love, You give

Always

Why do you feel this way,
Like you're lost in a maze?
You've searched for an answer to each rainy day
But somehow you end up dismayed;
Mountains arise on your sides,
Seems there's no place to hide
And though you may know,
I just want you to know
That I am that one place to abide;

When you're frightened and scared
In the enemy's lair
Remember I'll always be here,
To shower you down with My love
And to show you how much I care

Maybe you don't realise;
You're the apple of My eye
Your name is engraved on the palm of My hand
You are the reason I died;
My love for you is so deep
Goes beyond what any eye can see
So, though you can't see Me physically
My presence with you is so real;

When you're hurting inside,
Makes Me want to cry
A feeling I cannot deny;
So, no matter what you're going through
I will always be here for you

You can lean on Me, child
And I'll show you a love that is
Tender, gentle and mild
Coming straight from My heart;
When the friends that you know
They pick up and go
I will always be here for you

Always Near

A friend so dear, who's always there
Is really kinda hard to find,
I've searched in places far and near
Maybe I was blind;

But somehow, I know I wasn't wrong
There is only one of You,
Who's ever near, my life to share
J-E-S-U-S, I love You

A life with You, so real and true
Full of joy and happiness,
A love beyond compare;
And where You are
Is where I always want to be
Resting in Your arms for eternity

Somehow I know I can't go wrong
When I'm walking hand in hand with You;
Please hold me tight, every day and night
Lord, I just want to be with You

You stick so close to me
You're always there
You make my life so sweet
You're always near

When I awake to the morning light
You're there, my Love so dear;
Peace I find in Your caring arms
I know You're always near;
And when I lay me down to sleep
There's no need for me to fear
Because You're watching over me;
I know You're always near

By Fire

Elijah and four fifty prophets of Baal
All the people of Israel
They gathered together at Ahab's call
On top of Mount Carmel;
Elijah threw the challenge
And the people all agreed
So, the prophets prepared their sacrifice
And called on Baal to heed

"Baal, answer us", the prophets cried
But Baal did not heed
"Baal, answer us", they cried even louder
Who knows, maybe he was asleep;
But, Baal did not answer
Baal didn't do a thing
So, Elijah prepared his sacrifice
And called on The Mighty King

Almighty Warrior,
Creator of the heavens and the earth
Almighty Lord of Hosts
In You alone, I make my boast;
All the universe declares Your praise
They praise and magnify Your Holy name
Mighty in battle, Ancient of days
You will ever be the same

The God who answers by fire
The God through Whom power flows;
Almighty, victorious in battle,
There's no other God that I know
Who answers by fire!

A Little Touch

There was a story of a lady,
Who had a flow of blood
For twelve long years,
Seen all the doctors all around her,
Spending everything
But none could meet her need;

So with tears in her eyes,
On her knees she cried,
Looking up above for a solution;
But, then she heard that Jesus was around,
And her faith began to rise;
So, she said to herself,
If I can get through the crowd,
If I can just touch His robe;
He doesn't even have to know

Just a little touch
And He healed her
Just a little touch
And then she was made whole;
Just a little touch
And He saved her;
If you can just believe,
Just a little touch is all you need!

There was a man called Bartimaeus,
He was blind,
They say he could not see;
Every day he took his place by the wayside,
Begging:
"A nickel or a dime, anything, please help me"

Unusual commotion,
Excitement filled the air;
So, he asked,
"What's going on out there?"
And they said,
"Jesus Christ is passing by!"
So, he threw off his cloak,
In faith, he arose,
He shouted so loud,
"Lord, please save me now!"

Just a little touch
And He healed him
Just a little touch
And then he was made whole,
Just a little touch
And He saved him;
If you can just believe,
Just a little touch is all you need!

Got to Trust

In times of greatest struggle
When the angry billows roll
You can always count on Jesus
He's the anchor for your soul;
And if you trust Him at all times
You're bound to enjoy
Hope, peace and comfort
And the fulness of joy

I may not know what you're going through
I may not know your needs
But one thing that I know
Is that Jesus cares indeed;
Things may look complicated
The future may look dim
But He will make a way
If you put your trust in Him

You've got to trust,
Just trust Him,
Trust in the Lord your God
And He will grant you
The desires of your heart;
Nothing is impossible
If you only lean on Him;
So, you've got to trust,
Just trust Him,
Trust in the Lord your God
And He will grant you
The desires of your heart

My Trust

Father, in You, will I trust
You alone are faithful and just;
When the troubles of life
Try to push me to the wall
I'll hold on tight;
In Your arms, I can't fall

My Refuge, my Protector
Nothing's too hard for You,
My shelter from the storm
I put my trust in You

I Believe

So many times
We face trials and tribulations
Everything's so difficult
Everywhere's so dark;
The pain we feel,
The struggle with our will
Creates a burden heavy,
A wound so hard to heal;

But You said we should bring our burdens
And lay them at Your feet
You want to heal the pain we feel inside;
Everything is possible
There's nothing You can't do
If from our hearts we say, "I believe."

I believe
Help my unbelief;
I know that You can do it
But at times, it's hard to see;
Lord, I know,
But at times inside me, I say, "No."
I want to trust You daily;
It's all I want to do

Mountains high,
It's another situation
How do you get over?
How do you get by?
You've tried all ways,
But you're still stuck in the same place
It just looks so impossible
To keep the Christian pace;

But You said we should bring our burdens
And lay them at Your feet
You want to heal the pain we feel inside;
Everything is possible
There's nothing You can't do
If from our hearts we say, "I believe."

I believe
Help my unbelief;
I know that You can do it
But at times, it's hard to see;
Lord, I know,
But at times inside me, I say, "No."
I want to trust You daily;
It's all I want to do

I Stand

Thinking of the goodness of Jesus
Pondering His loving kindness
Remembering all He's done for me,
Takes me back to Calvary,
Where He gave His life that I may live
Shed His blood to set me free
Defeated the enemy
That I might live victoriously

And now, because of Jesus
I've got all it takes to run this race;
All because of Jesus
I can fight the good fight of faith

Jesus, You are so good
Nothing is too hard for You to do
Your love for us is everlasting;
You're the Solid Rock
On You, I stand

Nothing is too hard for God to do
Living in Him means He lives in you;
So, though the devil tries to get you down
Failure is his if you stand your ground;
You're more than a conqueror
Never give up,
You're an overcomer
When you're standing on The Rock

Now, because of Jesus
You've got all it takes to run this race
All because of Jesus
You can fight the good fight of faith

Jesus, You are so good
Nothing is too hard for You to do
Your love for us is everlasting;
You're the Solid Rock
On You, I stand

If You're Missing
(for Christmas)

On the very first Christmas day
My True Love gave to me
A precious little treasure
Wrapped in love and royalty;
It didn't seem much at the time
But today, it's plain to see
That Jesus, You're the One
Who gives this season true meaning

Even though I see the snowflakes fall
And hear the melody of sweet carols,
There's no Christmas time if You're missing;
I can have myself a Christmas tree,
Open presents with my family
But it's still not Christmas day if You're missing

Hey over there, sad and gloomy
Wipe those tears away,
I need you just to listen up
To what I have to say;
Jesus knows what you're going through
And He can make a way,
But He needs you to remember
That you're the reason why He came

So, even though I see the snowflakes fall
And hear the melody of sweet carols,
There's no Christmas time if You're missing;
I can have myself a Christmas tree,
Open presents with my family
But it's still not Christmas day if You're missing

Wonderful, Counsellor, Prince of Peace,
Your love will never cease;
Manger-born,
Humble King of kings
Knowing You makes Christmas time complete

Even though I see the snowflakes fall
And hear the melody of sweet carols,
There's no Christmas time if You're missing;
I can have myself a Christmas tree,
Open presents with my family
But it's still not Christmas day if You're missing

There's no Christmas day
It fades away
Lord, if You're missing!

No Christmas

There's no Christmas,
Without You, Jesus
There's no Christmas
Lord, if You're not here;
You came, You died
Gave Your life as a sacrifice;
Out of love for me
You shed precious blood on the tree;
I could never repay
All the things You've done for me
But I'm grateful Lord because You came,
You died and rose again;
Lord, I'm grateful because You came

Hand in Hand
(Our Song)

I love you, and you love me
And that's the way it should be
This love we share
Will always shine so bright and clear,
Conquering all fear

So, when the storms of this life
Try to stir up our lives
Stronger we will stand in Christ;
Through thick and through thin
We are a winning team
'Cos the Greater One is on our side

Together, you and I, hand in hand
On Jesus our cornerstone, we'll stand
Reigning together in this life
Helping each other to the heights;
This love we share will never wax cold
Stronger and stronger, it will grow;
Together, hand in hand, you and I
We will live a life of happiness and joy

Apple of Your Eye

Lord I know
That You will not forsake me;
Lord I know
That You will never leave me;
Lord I know
That You will ever love me;
I am the apple of Your eye

True Love

A love that is so caring
A love that is so kind
A love that is so loving
A love that blows my mind

A love so peculiar
A love beyond compare
A love with no restrictions
A love that's always there

A love that is unending
A love that never fails
A love that's unconditional
A love that never grows stale

A love that heals my broken heart
And fills it up with glee;
A love that has its being
Through shed blood at Calvary

A love that is unearnable
Priceless it is indeed;
A love that flows from up above
That's the love He has for me!

Love Made Me

It's interesting;
We believe we can make love
When actually, love made us
We think it's hidden in emotions and feelings
And shown through actions and words;
But it's more than what we say or feel
So much more than what we do,
True love is bigger than any of us;
Father, true love is You!

The more I look into Your word
The more it's clear to me,
That true love is truly You
And You made me

You gave Your Son who had it all
To take the sin and shame
Of someone who had nothing at all
Yep, I'm talking about me

Father, I can't thank You enough
For all You've done for me
When I was blind and lost
You shone so I could see;
When I turned my back on You
You still stayed by my side
Father, You never left me
Even when I tried to hide

You took away my darkness
Replaced it with Your Light
What manner of love is this?
It truly blows my mind

No greater love have I seen
Than the love You have for me;
Father, You are love
And I'm so glad that
Love made me

Love...Set Me Free

There was man
A peculiar man;
A man who cared
A man who loved the world,
He went about doing good
His name was Jesus Christ.
He gave His life for all mankind,
He gave His life that we may all be free;
He rose again that we may live
And live victoriously

All because of love
He shed his blood
To set us free from the enemy
I'm so glad, and I'm so grateful
His love has set me free

In case you didn't know this already
Jesus Christ died for everybody
His life He gave for you and me
That we might live eternally
But then, you must have figured
It isn't automatic,
You play your part or simply forget it;
Confess Him with your lips
With Your heart beliving,
That's what you need to do
If you want to receive Him

And don't go thinking
That you're just too dirty,
Jesus can cleanse anybody
If you're still breathing,
Then it's not too late
He will take you in no matter your state;
So give up your life
Place it in His hands
And He will make you
A brand new man

Death or life?
It's your choice to make;
But, please think carefully
Don't make a mistake;
If you aren't blind
Then it's clear to see,
Only His love
Can set you free

All because of love
He shed his blood
To set us free from the enemy
I'm so glad, and I'm so grateful
His love has set me free

Love, So Real

At times I feel I'm all alone
At times I feel real low
And even the darkness of the shining sun
Looks so dim;
When all the hurt, the pain, I feel inside
Brings me to my knees
Knowing You're there for me
through thick and thin
Gives me peace

What would I do without Your love
That gives me strength to carry on;
Without Your shoulder there to lean on
Each time I cry;
Without Your arms around to hug me tight,
To keep me warm on a stormy night;
I know the love You give
Is so real

So many times, I've strayed,
I've walked away
Tried to live life all alone
Somehow I thought
I wouldn't need a helping hand;
So many times I've failed You,
I've acted like a fool
Felt like hiding away,
But still, You took me in
And wiped away my shame

What would I do without Your love
That gives me strength to carry on;
Without Your shoulder there to lean on
Each time I cry;
Without Your arms around to hug me tight,
To keep me warm on a stormy night;
I know the love You give
Is so real

You shower me with a love so real
You hold me close and tight,
And being here in Your presence
Gives me peace of mind;
Each time You touch this heart of mine
With Your warm embrace
It makes me want to love You more
Each and every day

What would I do without Your love
That gives me strength to carry on;
Without Your shoulder there to lean on
Each time I cry;
Without Your arms around to hug me tight,
To keep me warm on a stormy night;
I know the love You give
Is so real

Someday
(for Beautiful Betty)

It's hard to believe you're no longer here
I can still hear your voice so loud, so clear;
It's hard to believe you're not here with us
I can still feel your touch,
The tender love you showered on us;
The life and joy you bring when you're around,
I'll never forget your loving smile,
And even though I wish I could hold your hand
I know you're safe in God's loving arms

I'll always remember your loving care
Freely you gave of yourself, always there to help;
And how could I forget your listening ear
Always so near,
My friend until the very end;
You made me realise no height was too high
I can reach for the skies with God on my side;
Beautiful mama, it's so hard to let you go
But this one thing I know

Someday, one day
I'll see your smiling face
I'll feel your warm embrace;
Someday, one day
I may not know the day,
But I'll see you once again

My every thought of you is fond and so sweet
Memories of you, mama, I'll forever keep
And though I love and miss you so
I know that we will meet,
We'll meet again at Jesus' feet

Someday, one day
I'll see your smiling face
I'll feel your warm embrace;
Someday, one day
I may not know the day,
But I'll see you once again

O mama, how I miss you so
So hard to see you go
But now you're walking down the streets of gold
In the presence of the Lord;
One day I'll see your smile again
Hand in hand, walking down again,
Walking down the streets of gold
In the presence of the Lord

Out of Sight

"Out of sight is out of mind"
But what about if I were blind?
I'd use my other senses to see
And discern if something were fine or ugly;
Character would shine to me so bright,
While looks would simply fade out of sight

"Out of sight is out of mind"
Goes far beyond what the eye can find;
Both those with eyes and those without
Have eyes to see; there is no doubt
Most use lenses, a few use the heart
But the latter to me is better by far

"Out of sight is out of mind"
Makes no difference, with eyes or blind;
The truth of this quote, at least to me,
Is that,
The heart always tells the true story!

Ponder

At times I sit back and ponder
If Jesus hadn't come for me;
But He came, He suffered, He died
And most of all, He rose again;
With His blood, He set me free

Now I have abundant life
In a measure that can't be measured;
I speak the word, the devil flees;
The Greater One resides in me

Remember,
You're the dwelling of the Holy Ghost
The Spirit of God lives in you
So, when things look dim
Trust the One within,
He's your guide,
Your counsellor,
Your friend!

So, no matter what the devil says
Or what he tries to do
Remember,
Jesus came, He suffered, He died;
And rose again just for you

Keep Pressing On

Have you ever felt like no one loves you
Have you ever felt like no one really cares
Or does it look like your life is full of failures
Everything you face seems too hard to bear?

Remember, with Jesus
There is always a way
Just keep trusting with each passing day;
You've been made more than a conqueror
Through the blood of the Son,
So forget all past failures
And keep pressing on!

So, when that scum bag comes to tell you
"You won't make it through the day"
Simply fix your gaze on Jesus
With Him, there's always a way

Place your trust in Jesus
And see what He will do;
In every situation
He will see you through

Because with Jesus
There is always a way
Just keep trusting with each passing day
You've been made more than a conqueror
Through the blood of the Son
So forget all past failures
And keep pressing on!

Make A Way

Toiling through the night
And still no hope in sight
Deep inside your heart
You need the strength to carry on;
Like you're lost within a maze,
Your life's in disarray,
You're searching for that Somebody
To show you the way

The way to go, even though
It seems you're all alone;
A ray of hope, a shining light
In the darkness of your night;
To let you know, it may be tough
But no matter what you're going through
He'll be there to make a way for you

He will make a way
Turn your night to day,
Here you when you call
In the time of storm
When you're all alone;
He will make a way,
He will wipe your tears away;
He'll hear you when you pray;
God will make a way

Lean On Him

Over two thousand years ago
Jesus died for you and me,
He shed His blood and rose again
And gave us the victory

Now we're more than conquerors
The overcomer lives within,
We live a life victorious
When we lean on Him

And when life's light looks a little dim
And the devil says, "you can't win."
When all hope seems to fade away
Remember, never, ever give in!

Because, when the pressures of life
Try to cage you in,
It's not time to quit
But to lean on Him

No One Else

The mountain looks so high
How can I make it to the other side?
And looking all around me
No one who can help can I see;
But when all hope seemed lost
And I was headed for the dust
Jesus gently picked me up

Now, when I'm hit on all sides
Like a boat amid a storm,
Or faced with situations
That seem impossible,
I do not fear
Neither do I cry,
Because the Greater One
Is always by my side

Why You love me so
I will never know,
But I'm so grateful
For a love, unconditional;
And with everything within me
This one thing I pledge to do
To put my trust in no one else,
In no one else but You

The One

When tragedy comes your way
When all hope seems to fade
When you look all around
And there's no help to be found
Jesus says, "Just come,
Bring your burdens, bring every one",
And He will give you rest
Turn to dust every test

When the devil comes your way
Tries to mess up your day
There's no need to fear
Just remember, Jesus is near;
In Him, you are made strong
He's on your side all day long
And He will never let you go
If you will only hold on

He is the one
To whom all things are possible,
No matter what it may be
The Saviour holds the key;
He is the one
Who can meet your every need,
And if you trust in Him
He will surely bring you through

So when the devil tries to pull you down
Remember, the Greater One is always around;
He's there to help
If you ask Him to,
Just trust Him
And see what He will do

He is the one
To whom all things are possible,
No matter what it may be
The Saviour holds the key;
He is the one
Who can meet your every need,
And if you trust in Him
He will surely bring you through

Peace

Burdens so heavy, driving you crazy
Everything looks the wrong way round;
The cares of this life weigh you down
Turning your smile into a frown,
Hope gradually diminishes
As darkness replaces light

But if you look above
You'll see a ray of love
Shining from the Father
To the depths of your soul;
His arms are open wide
Calling you to abide,
'Cos here in His presence
Is all the peace you need

His burden's not heavy
And His yoke is easy
Down on your knees
You can find true peace;
He hears when you say,
"Father, please show me the way.
My life is in disarray
Shine Your light on me."

And if you look above
You'll see a ray of love
Shining from the Father
To the depths of your soul;
His arms are open wide
Calling you to abide
'Cos here in His presence
Is all the peace you need

All the peace you need
Is under the shadow of His wings

On My,, Inside

I rise to the top
And there I stay
Because I am the head
I am not the tail

Amongst my neighbours
I shine like a star
I am more excellent than them
By far

On the earth's high places
That's where I ride
Because The Greater One
Lives on my inside

Sweet Spirit

Made in His image
And His likeness too
You have His sweet Spirit
Living in you;
To counsel and help;
He's always there
To comfort and lead;
Your burdens He'll bear

Things to come;
He'll show if you ask,
What you don't understand
He'll take away the mask;
So ask Him to guide you
Each and every day
And you'll come out tops
In this Christian race

Waiting for You

Quite sometime ago
A man called Jesus came to sow,
His precious life He gave for us
On the cross;
He died for you and me
To give us life, to set us free
That we may have the victory
Over the enemy

But we've got to give up our lives
And surrender all to Him;
Open up our fragile hearts
And let the Saviour in

Jesus is the way;
He is the truth and the light
By no one else can we be saved
But by Him;
So, why waste your time
On the wrong side of life
Why not open your heart and let Him in?
He's waiting for you

I guess we all know this world isn't home
When we die, there's somewhere else to go
Heaven or hell? Take your pick
You want some advice?
You better choose quick;
'Cos the time is nigh when the Saviour will come
Covered in glory
To take His children home

Jesus is calling;
He's ringing your bell
Will you leave Him outside
Or let Him in now;
Make up your mind,
What are you going to do?
He won't wait forever
But He's still waiting for you!

Jesus is the way
He is the truth and the light
By no one else can we be saved
But by Him;
So, why waste your time
On the wrong side of life,
Why not open your heart and let Him in?
He's waiting for you

Where You Belong

Why do you try to hide?
I see behind your disguise,
The worries that keep you awake at night,
I feel what you're feeling inside;
Don't you know
That My love for you is unconditional?
So, place your heart in My hands
And I'll never let you go

Call on My name,
And I'll be right there;
When you fall, just take My hand
And I'll take you there;
To a place where you'll be safe
There's no need to fear;
A place where My love overflows,
And there are pleasures
Like you've never known,
In My presence,
That's where you belong

I see those tears fill your eyes,
I've watched you run without no place to hide;
And even when good friends let you down,
I need you to know that I'm always around;
Don't you know that My love for you
Will never, ever, never, ever cease?
And though you may not understand
I just need you to trust in Me

Call on My name,
And I'll be right there;
When you fall, just take My hand
And I'll take you there;
To a place where you'll be safe
There's no need to fear;
A place where My love overflows,
And there are pleasures
Like you've never known,
In My presence,
That's where you belong

The night may seem dark
And the mountain so high,
My child, don't worry
I'm right by your side;
The storm may be fierce
And the valley so wide
But my child, don't worry
I'm right by your side

So, call on My name,
And I'll be right there;
When you fall, just take My hand
And I'll take you there;
To a place where you'll be safe
There's no need to fear;
A place where My love overflows,
And there are pleasures
Like you've never known,
In My presence,
That's where you belong

Watching Over You

When you're down and feeling low
And it seems you're all alone
It may look like the end is nigh
But don't give up, He's by your side:
God is watching over you!

So, there's no need for you to fear
Just remember, God is near
Your prayers He will surely hear
Your burden He will always bear:
He is watching over you!

The Word

The word of God is the light
That puts all darkness to flight
It also gives us insight
Into the things of the Father

The word of God is a mirror
Reflecting Jesus' picture
Through the word
We'll attain the full stature
Of the Son of the Father

The word of God is alive
It is the truth; it has no lies
It is a fountain of wisdom
A mine of wealth,
Without it, we can't survive;
But if you let it flood your mind
And if you let it rule your heart
It will guide you along His chosen way
The life-eternal path

Victory

There was a time when I felt so hurt inside
Nothing about me was going right,
Everyone around seemed to turn their backs on me
And I asked myself, "Why me?"

Day after day, life grew darker still
When it came to sadness, I had my fill,
Life without hope was all I could see
And I asked myself, "Why me?"

But in the midst of my darkness
Jesus came to me
I asked Him into my life; He set me free
And with the Spirit of God
On the inside of me
I have nothing else
But victory

So, if you feel something's missing in your life
And you need the light to shine inside
Jesus is the answer; He is the way
So, why not let him in; It's never too late

And in the midst of your darkness
He will come to you
If you ask Him in, He'll see you through
And the Spirit of God
Will take His place inside of you
And you will have nothing else
But victory!

Faith

Faith is the evidence of things not seen,
You don't see,
Yet you do believe;
Faith is the substance of things hoped for,
You need faith
If you want to be sure
of success
In this Christian race,
So many trials you will have to face,
But walking by faith and not by sight,
Your future is more than bright

That is why we have to live a life of faith;
It is the victory
That overcomes the world,
Faith will make a way for you and me
In this troubled world;
Make it a way of living
And your life will start changing
Into the person of Jesus;
We have got to live by faith

Only One Way

There is only one way to heaven
Through Jesus Christ the Son
And if you make Him Lord of your life
You will make heaven your home

Heaven is home; heaven is home
That's what everybody loves to say
But they seem to forget one important fact:
To heaven, there is only one way

The only way is to be born again
Through Jesus Christ the Son
For He alone can save your soul
Jesus is the only one

For God loved the world so very much
That He gave His only son
To add a marvellous touch,
To all the world,
To all humanity
That we may be one
And reign with Him

For two thousand years back
On Calvary's cross
Jesus Christ died for all of us
The darkness in our lives
He took upon Himself
Just because He loves us
He delivered us from filth

So, confess Him with your lips
Believe in your heart
Accept Jesus Christ;
He guarantees a new start

Have that personal relationship
With the One who died for you
Make Him number one
In everything you do;
He'll help, He'll guide
With Him, you'll overcome
He's your Saviour, your Friend
With Him, the victory is won

There is only one way to heaven
Through Jesus Christ the Son
And if you make Him Lord of your life
You will make heaven your home

Give Your Life

Some time, someday
In a twinkle of an eye
The Lord is coming for His own;
The hour is unknown
When we will all go home
But will home be heaven or hell?
Death or life
The choice is yours to make,
Life is heaven,
But you must be born again

To reign victorious
You need Jesus in your life
He alone can set you free;
The hour is not too late
For you to make that change
Just place your heart in His loving arms
Death or life
The choice is yours to make,
Life is heaven,
But you must be born again

Years ago on Calvary's cross
Jesus shed His blood for all of us;
In the world today,
No greater love has ever been displayed;
Don't let it be in vain
Give your life to Him today

Let Him In

Maybe you're there, and about to crack
Each step forward just takes you back
Nights full of tears flowing from your eyes
A pain so deep, impossible to disguise
You look all around for a glimmer of hope
It almost feels like the end of the road
But wait a second, don't give up yet
Let me tell you about someone I met

They call Him Jesus,
You may have heard of Him
He's the One who gave His life
So that you and I may live;
The One who took your pain
With each slash upon His back
The One who says, "I love you"
Even when you don't love Him back;
The One who wrote your name
On the palm of His hand
He even knows the hairs on your head
Yes, every strand
See, He loves you unconditionally;
He'll love you till the end
And though He's the Messiah
He says you can call Him Friend

So, though you're feeling all forlorn
And it seems as if all hope is gone,
Jesus says He'll carry you through
If you only let Him in!

Revival

Father,
I call on Your name
I humbly bow, and I pray
For though darkness may seem
To cover the land
I can sense the dawn of a new day

So, I lift up my voice and say
For revival in our land, I pray,
Every contrary spirit has got to bow
As You rule in this land once again

Let Your kingdom come
Let Your will be done,
Take the hearts of kings
Align them with Your will;
I see You lifted high
Your glory floods the sky
As Your reign takes over once again
Father, on my knees I say,
For revival Lord, I pray

More

I need You, sweet Spirit
More and more in my life,
To guide me and show me
How to do things aright

How I need You
More;
I really need You
More;
So much I need You
More;
More and more

Outro

Well, I think I better stop here, or I might go on forever. Thank you for taking the time to read the pages of this book. I hope you have been blessed by every word.

My prayer is, and always will be, that these words will be as real to you as they are to me.

Bye for now
~ *akin.o.*~